Gold
Country

Other Books by Shirley Kaufman

The Floor Keeps Turning

> 1969 United States Award of the International Poetry Forum and National Council on the Arts Selection

Translations

My Little Sister

> Translated from the Hebrew of Abba Kovner in *Abba Kovner and Nelly Sachs: Selected Poems*

A Canopy in the Desert

> Translated from the Hebrew of Abba Kovner

Gold Country

SHIRLEY KAUFMAN

University of Pittsburgh Press

Library of Congress Cataloging in Publication Data

Kaufman, Shirley.
  Gold country.

  (Pitt poetry series)
  Poems.
  1. Title.
  PS3561.A862G6   811' .5'4   73–5542
  ISBN 0–8229–3269–5
  ISBN 0–8229–5238–6 (pbk.)

Acknowledgment is made to the following publications in which some of these poems first appeared: *The American Poetry Review, Field, The Iowa Review, Kayak, "Mark in Time: Portraits & Poetry/San Francisco," The Massachusetts Review, Midstream, The Nation, New American Review, Poetry, Poetry Northwest, Quarterly Review of Literature, Today's Poets (Chicago Tribune Magazine)*, and *Voyages*.

"Apples," "Getting There," "In Touch," and "The Dream" were first published in *Poetry*.

"Where" first appeared in *The American Poetry Review*, Vol. 2, No. 4.

"Realities" was originally published in *"Mark in Time: Portraits & Poetry/San Francisco"* © 1971 by Glide Publications.

The quotations appearing in "After the Voices" are from *Voices* by Antonio Porschia, translated by W. S. Merwin. Copyright 1969 by William S. Merwin. Reprinted with the permission of Follett Publishing Company, a division of Follett Corporation.

To the memory of my mother

Contents

I

Driving on the San Diego Freeway   3
Where   4
Gold Country   6
After the Voices   9
Realities   19
Getting There   21
Reading the Tarot   23
Miracles   24
After Woodstock   25
The Hoopoe Bird   27
Amherst: One Day, Five Poets   28

II

Wonders   33
Summer   34
Seeing You in a Dream   38
Apples   40
Nechama   42
Sorrow, Sorrow   45
Jerusalem Notebook   47
The Burning of the Birds   58

Contents

III

Gone with the Popcorn	63
Poem for a Gemini	65
Head	66
In Touch	67
Signs	68
The Performance	69
Subversion	71
Feeding Time in the Lion House	72
The Dream	73
Michal	74
Giving	75
For Joan at Eilat	79

I

Looking for gold . . .

Driving on the San Diego Freeway

What if the cars stopped
running motors
all over the world
the wheels stopped
turning as if
they had never been
discovered we walked
slowly finding
our feet our legs
as far as we could
go land's end
the edge of the ocean
up to our lips
and found each moving
part of ourselves
our lives again
at the beginning
coming out of that
wet our skin still
shining with water
and our breath.

Where

You are sitting on the edge
of our bed naked
leaning over your knees
your elbows resting
on them and your palms
cupping your face

you do not know me
speaking to your back
naked I speak to the light
along your spine
your smooth shoulders

wondering if you turn
your face perhaps
it will belong
to somebody else
perhaps the woman
lying here
will not be me

what we imagine
is
in some real place
but where

Degas said an artist
finds a hand so beautiful
he can shut himself in a room
the rest of his life
and paint fingernails

the smallest part
but every day to discover
what he knows

After the Voices

from the aphorisms of Antonio Porchia
translated by W. S. Merwin

1

All that I have lost I find at every
step, and remember that I have lost it.

Grass. It all comes separate
in shining pieces when I
lie down in it.

The humming
begins. Damp, inhabited caves
I had forgotten, huge bones
no longer waltzing.

Games
in the dark, that bearded
saint turned serpent,
redeemable only with kisses
under the fern.

I entertain
myself, a carrion in the weeds,
feeder and fed-upon.

But the small girl
rocking in my joints won't
be absolved. She keeps
catching moths, watching them
smother in a jar.

2

A great deal that I no longer continue,
within myself, continues there on its own.

> All night long I give away your suits,
> wool at my fingers, jointed,
> having their own seams,
> putting the cat outside.
>
> I stay behind the window
> watching us run.
>
>   What you send
> back to me bounces
> against a net. Trees bend
> to scratch their shadows.
> Water flows.
>
>   And pride.
> How it sits there like dust
> on the shutters.
> Infects the air.

3

When everything is finished, the mornings are sad.

Waking is not the same.
The half-blind woman tears leaves
from the rock and tosses them
in the water. Anise. A weed.
I lay the fragrance to your skin.

Nothing goes on. Except the dead.
Except the crumbs we sweep
under the rug.

          The smooth,
flat rock you skipped three
times in the sea.

4

The chains that bind us most closely
are the ones we have broken.

When the ground crumbles
under our house and the storm
moves down the gutters and gales
loosen the roof, we let go.

The clock stops, stunned where we are
locked in our arms inside the case
and toppling over.

And if
I reach the open
from the pendulum's box, escape
the knocking of bronze,
and in a raging wind recover
my breath,

why
does your face define my fingers,
why do we move against our mouths
into our mouths' dark habit, why
does the throat's soft ticking
make perilous lies?

Would there be this eternal seeking
if the found existed?

Someone comes up to you keeping
his hands closed. He goes
to everyone. "What have I got
in my hand?"
               You think
that what you want most
must be hidden there. Right one
or left. You beg him
to open his fist.

               And finally
he does. Look how the skin
lies curdled in his palm.

6

The loss of a thing affects us
until we have lost it altogether.

And here I am in the kitchen
not knowing why.

What
if we know the play
is not a play?

I am the one
who got up from that chair.

What did you do today?

I cut my hair I drove
the car into a ditch
I broke my leg.

Where did you hide the ladder?

Meat loaf again.

I forget where I put the key.
I forget your name.

We tear life out of life
to use it for looking at itself.

I roll my domestic head
in the whole hive of your bees.
They sting out my eyes.
They are blacker than words.
I am still alive.

My own voices saying
kill, kill.

Time
to stop being who you
think you are.

My long bones shine
as in an X ray
out of their meat.

8

We see by something which illumines
us, which we do not see.

Two gulls unlatch their wings
letting it in,
                    sunlight
a wafer between your teeth.

I see you row out
on the bay. You lift
a loneliness of oars, call
and your calling baits a line,
calling to catch.

Under reflected suns I hear you
where I partly stroke (my feet
are fish, gills from my ankles
breathing).

            Salmon quiver
under the surface of your smile.

When I look for my existence
I do not look for it in myself.

Lemon in blossom
and smaller than leaves soft
wings at the heart of it

closing and breathing,
the sun easing
into the flower.

Castle of hills seen
far in the distance.
We are inside it,

light and the darkness
together and moving
along the wall.

Believable,
arranged around us
when you slide from me.

A moisture
on mirrors giving
us back our breath.

10

I know what I have given you. I
do not know what you have received.

I am combing my hair at the top
of the glass mountain.

A steep slope
of language
zigzags
from me to you.

You will break
your neck on it.

You know exactly
what you have said.

You do not
know what I have heard.

Realities

for George Oppen

When I've been warm
a long time, I don't think of any
fever in the absence of wind,
hum of a few bees, orange cat
dozing in the sun.

　　　　　　The idea
I have of myself is the thing
that's corrupted. To move
from that,

　　　　　　　turning down sheets
at night, the skin
shines on the knuckles, fingers
pull at the fabric. Arm's swing,
shift of the elbow, stretch
at the wrist. Alive. My self
and nobody's mother.

The rest is comment.

　　　　　　Or
one could say: stars
grass the mountain
letting them be.

But we continue,
"Yes, I see," meaning
not what the eye takes in
but what we know along with it

Realities

or maybe after
when we look again.

The way I hold this prism
to the sun

            turning it sideways
to refract the light

until I see the rainbow
not the glass
the seven colors passing
through my hand.

Getting There

1

We go. Simply because it's there
for us to go to. Walk
on the surface, having to raise dust
where we never were. And say
we did it. Finding excuses.

We need to own them.
Crusts of other worlds. Carrying
flags and chocolate, comforts of home.

Whatever density we pass through,
pulsing and odd, we stake
our claim to, leaving
our garbage, giving names.

In our own language. Nothing
can stop us now.

2

Stonehenge is not a member
of the family. Not truth.
Though it is obvious enough.
Light ripens over the same place
every year. Tells how new we are,
how strange it is to look for God.

Only the rites change. Sun.
The moon. The old confusion
of the mind that keeps constructing
frames to put them in.

Suppose these ruins were standing
tall in Florida. Thousands of years
from now. Tourists will come
to marvel how we built, how
we pushed buttons in the desperate
brain, flinging ourselves to heaven
righteously, looking for stars
or holiness again.

Reading the Tarot

You tell me
the cup that's missing is the one
that counts. Turning away
from what one has.
Contentment. Even the moon
at dawn remembers the night before.
Still warm and rosy
underneath my cloak.

And it's the Queen of Pentacles
I choose. Good wife.
Good earth. She holds
it like the smooth skull
of an unborn child.

But the wing
on her head is the flight
her mind takes
somewhere
            another landscape
and an empty cup.

Miracles

Keep happening

                 oh less
than we would like them to.
They shrink
like cheap material in the wash
puckered by history

                     even
with all those believers
continents of excited women
empirical children
eating brown rice.

But it would take
so many now
saviors
just as wonderful in life
as they're reported after.

Ask any specialist
in ecstasy
he'll falsify
the facts because
they matter.

                 Someone
is always on the way
to end the world
restoring Paradise.

After Woodstock

Her face breaking all over
in little pieces standing up shouting
shit man yeah yeah shaking her hair
like feathers in the dark the man
on the screen splits into three
jerking his arms his legs his neck
three heads six hands now squeeze
the cool sound between his fingers
squeeze the snakes out of his guitar
and three round mouths moan love ya
in the mike pressing it like three
women to his lips

               and leather
rocking smooth in front out of electric
funnels   beads

               they slap the seats
they bounce around me break down fences
to the launching pad

                   under their plastic
blankets in the rain slide down
the mud laughing mud in your eyes
your ears there lies the future
but you can't get hold of it sliding
and sliding in the mud

              loving
they call it loving
city bodies naked in the pond
nursing babies while the sun
beats time it's bright
and no one's fighting
in tall grass beside the field
they are taking their clothes off

slowly his pants her blouse his
socks her bra the music insists we can
hear it white flesh now the high
notes grow red grow purple
stain my whole mouth like berries
under the sky they are
berries hundreds of thousands
of berries swaying with their hair.

Shall I let my teeth sail out of my head
higher hug the drummer higher
do handstands on my seat higher shall I
tear up my passport and my credit cards
make my own music out of the dead
years amplified higher come back come
back cut my sleeves into fringes
fly

   out of it   suddenly
it's over and the last sound goes
like a stone dropped into water I can't
find it and the last endless garbage
catches fire and the last car
starts down the highway nothing is
certain only it

        happened

           there.

The Hoopoe Bird

The hoopoe bird has come back
with its feathered crown,
its tail strung black and white,
small as a hand.

It is the bird of Paradise come back
to the *kibbutz*, the only paradise
of optical illusion,
floating with trees.

Nobody's out of his head with fever,
and the bird hunts insects
after the fat mosquitoes,
skimming across the lawn.

It is the bird of Paradise
come back in summer, ebony and silver,
with the *shamir** dangling
out of its tiny beak.

It is the bird who whispered
in King Solomon's ears
secrets over the coo of doves
and farm machinery.

Now it begins all over,
and the hoopoe's flying
out of the old lost garden
while we run after it again.

* Mythical worm that split the rocks for
Solomon's Temple.

Amherst: One Day, Five Poets

1

Don when you drive me through the rain
into the woods the wet
leaves falling into leaves
I'm already high on soybeans.
Some people live on them like meat
or love
baked into loaves.

In that small house two poets
damp with leftover weather
the third who starts a fire
and brings small glasses
of his dandelion wine.
We sip it
slow
exhaling orange groves lemon trees.
The juice lights up our mouths.
"The citrus fruit," he says
and pours it out as one
who having everything to give
keeps giving it.

He wouldn't
think of it that way. And moves
through the warm steam of his giving
and gives us tea with rosemary.

And as we drink it looking up
from the bottom of our cups
or into them
we hear the rain
the burning logs
our swallowing.

2

The cupola is a windowed cage
at the top. The Holyoke Range
floats in the sky at twilight
and three half-dead wasps
blown in by the wind
jerk at my feet.
They can't get out again.
They wobble against the glass
and fall.

         Pale walls
the pale tatami floor.
Pearl jail she called it.
Safe as the inside of a shell.
Or wicker basket on her window sill.

She used to fill
it with her own warm gingerbread
and lower it to the children down below.

There is the recipe in her small script:
molasses sugar flour.
A branch of pear tree starts
to shine from the dark
the way a live thing moves
out of the stone
a hand releases to the light.

She wanted to know
if her poems breathed.

3

At Bradley Field
I'm looking for my plane to San Francisco
when the Russian poet arrives.
His mild face blooms like a star brought into focus
through a telescope
when he hears
where I'm headed for.
"My love!" he cries
meaning that I should give it
or it's mine
or that's how he feels about my city
"I'm yours!"

I turn once more to wave.
He shines like a face card out of the deck.
His joy runs over on his teeth
like an arc of light.
It dazzles me.
I'm yours I'm yours

then strapped in my seat
and home.

II

The gold light entering . . .

Wonders

When it was late
the Baal Shem Tov
set a tree on fire
to warm his friends
so they could leave their wagon
in the snow
and say the evening prayers
at the right time

merely by touching it.

Night will come on
before we get to the next town.

We make a place
for silence
in the dark

and your arms reach out
to hold me

for the small time
we have
by our own
light.

Summer

1

Water running and the sound
of birds

        tell what you don't
see but you can't be sure

it sings in the head
excessive

        like the fruit
all ripening at once

darts at my ears like feathers
small felt hammers on a xylophone

or the irrelevance of dancing
classical ballet

              the *entrechat*
up in the air the quick
heels meeting

           how many
times

      the air makes
passages for flight

the young girls turning
like white amaranth

               pure
motion of their fluttering
wrists

the birds fly
down on it and even silence
coming after us
with its own sound.

2

Once in Seattle when the ballet
came I watched
while Lichine made love
to a bird

covered with feathers
wings and plumes all gilded
hair gold neck gold
gauze like oil spilled over her

she spread her arms
took off and circled
my head

I saw her tongue
dart gold

before he leaped
in great arcs back of her
and stopped her
flight

I sat so close
that I could hear them
breathe

his gasping
as he lifted her

oh
nights I waited
in my bed: lovers
like dancers out of breath
the bird's shrill singing
in my blood

stretching my gold
wings out to him the tips
of feathers

parachutes
of birds oh lavish
le coq d'or!

3
You know it's summer when you're
into it

the peaches soften
in their skins

sun
on my hands like silk-lined
gloves

my wrists bend easy

as a bird

my eyelids
gold and my warm throat
the gold light entering
my veins

wings

    open

and he stops me rising
off the grass he's breathing
hard we

    dance.

Seeing You in a Dream

after Tu Fu

1

From the last place you traveled,
losing books, leaving
trains to go on without you,
drowning in dark bars you'd never
remember, I dreamed you
into my room.

There was a continent
filling with chairs.
If you stopped,
there were strangers'
faces.

2

These gulls that have risen
all day from the sea
may, like the exiled,
never return.

Two months now
I have thought of you
as tender, intimate and real
as though I am asleep.

Your fingers barely not
touching my arm, you tell me
your rides to undoing by water.
Over the side. And nights,
the child who climbs into your skin.

Not moving closer, you sigh
as if to breathe them
out of you.

Our city staggers
with fragrant women
while you are trying
not to be alone.

Thin books, a thousand years' fame,
and we, now that it's done?

Apples

No use waiting for it to stop
raining in my face like a wet towel
having to catch a plane,
to pick the apples from her tree
and bring them home.

The safest place to be
is under the branches. She
in her bed and her mouth
dry in the dry room.
Don't go out in the rain.

I stretch my arms for apples
anyway, feel how the ripe ones
slide in my hands like cups
that want to be perfect. Juices
locked up in the skin.

She used to slice them in quarters,
cut through the core,
open the inside out. Fingers
steady on the knife, expert
at stripping things.

Sometimes she split them sideways
into halves to let a star break
from the center with tight seeds,
because I wanted that,
six petals in the flesh.

Flavor of apples inhaled as flowers,
not even biting them.
Apples at lunch or after school
like soup, a fragrance rising
in the steam, eat and be well.

I bring the peeled fruit to her
where she lies, carve it
in narrow sections, celery white,
place them between her fingers,
Mother, eat. And be well.

Sit where her brown eyes
empty out the light, watching
her mind slip backwards
on the pillow, swallowing
apples, swallowing her life.

Nechama

They changed her name
to Nellie. All the girls.
To be American.
And cut her hair.

She couldn't give up
what she thought she lost.
Streets like ceiling cracks
she looked up watching
where the same boy bicycled always
to the gate of her Russian house.
She saw him tremble
in the steam over her tea
after the samovar was gone.
She was Anna Karenina
married to somebody else.

*

Oh she was beautiful. She could turn
into an egret with copper hair.
She could turn into a fig tree.
She could turn into a Siberian wolfhound.
She could turn into an opal
turning green. She could drown us
in the lake of her soft skin.

Rhythm of chopping garlic
motion as language in her wrists
warming her hands
rubbing it
over the leg of lamb.

*

Leaving the kitchen she would cry
over pictures telling us
nothing new

till the small light by her bed
kept getting lost under the blanket
where she crawled looking
for something she forgot
or money in her old house
under the hankies looking
for spare parts.

She swallowed what we brought
because we said to.

*

The rabbi knows
the 23rd psalm backwards
and he pretends he came for a wedding.

Do me a favor she still pleads
under the roses
begging for proof of faithfulness
or love. If I say yes
she might ask anything like
stay with me
or take me home.

*

It's my face staring
out of her picture
wrinkled and old
as a newborn infant

pushed there
ahead of myself

or memorizing lines
over and over in a soundproof room
until the smile is stuck there
and the lips stay frozen
like a hole in the ice
where a child fell in.

Sorrow, Sorrow

In Moscow there is a small cherry orchard
next to Chekhov's tomb. They put eggs
on graves to feed the souls.
We lie here flat between them
and the earth, and try to listen.
Something opens and shuts like my heart pumping.
They must be floating back for more.
Do they sit down to eat?
Do they stretch out their arms when we bring flowers?

Rain wakes me. I want
to fill the whole room with wet flowers.
I want to feel their slack tongues
sucking the light, the air.

I knock things over in the dark.
Souls, flowers, I give my breath up,
balancing eggs.
Old girls under water swimming
with inexhaustible strokes.

Only a diver moves freely
in every direction.
I get up tired.

One year. Two deaths.
Our mothers still on the porch
like the smell of autumn,
telling each other they're alive.
No one believes them.

Our fathers won't stop
crying for their wives.
They squeeze their tears
in a salt shoe and throw it
back and forth across the net.
They make us run for it.
Our only exercise.
They sit in our favorite chairs
and wipe their eyes.
Even our need
to grieve with them is suspect.
They keep the bodies to themselves.

I watch the leaves curl into their stems and go.
You moan in your sleep, still dreaming,
reach for the breast of your mother
in our bed. I was counting
the crooked tombstones on our lawn.
The mound of your hand on my skin
is the newest one.
I move in the hollow of your palm.
I crawl inside.

Jerusalem Notebook

1

And up again because
going is not enough
go *up* we say
into these hills

by which we exceed
ourselves.

Little stone heaps
glowing out of the old
bald rock
pitted with tombs

and valleys
like the tongue.

In the warm dark
stars
move into focus
and reflections
of stars

as if the stones send up
their whiteness.

2

An old man crosses
the road
thin ends of his beard
threads of the four corners
lift

and the dry bones.

We are all
leaning in the open
where the wind is

dust from the highway
travels blindly
back to the hills

something is up there
in the shanks
of the twisted olive trees

hanging on.

3

As in those medieval maps
the three known continents
open like petals
from a flower

scorched heart of the world
Jerusalem pushes
out of its own earth
at the top

      blind
in the huge light.

Sunrise. The bones
put on their flesh again

they have been getting
ready every day

confused by bells
and ram's horns

tape-recorded
cries.

4
Why did he tell me:
I'm afraid
to go.

The heavenly city
is on earth with balconies
the wash
turned inside out to dry.
They beat the rugs
and dirt flies
in the neighbor's socks.

Ruins break
into smaller pieces
where they are.

You can buy thorn crowns
in any size.

But to slice cucumbers
for breakfast
spreading the soft
white cheese

yielding to it
every day.

5

Not like the memories
first homes we lived in
stories our parents told us
we didn't hear.

A spider's web
across the entrance
to a cave means
someone is hiding there.

The dead lie under us
in layers
waiting to rise.

Even the cats.
They won't drown
in the four rivers
of paradise
they will fly
upward
with the rest.

6

These hills at sunset
turning copper
find their first shade.

Waking to color them again
each thing surrounds us
rosy with light. Our skin

is luminous.
Shadows run off your back
like oil
a shine of stones
in shallow water
under the sun.

Sun. Stones.
Strange faces of people
passing in the street

not to encounter
but to feel the weight
of them
pinning you down.

7

How can I look
at this sun?
Bring a black hen and tear it
lengthwise and crosswise
and shave the middle of your head
and put the bird on it
and leave it there until it sticks.

And if the sun
burns through me?
Go down to the river
stand in water
up to your neck
and then swim out and sit down.

And if I get chilled?
Rabbi Joseph cured it
by working at the mill
Rabbi Sheshet carried
heavy beams.

8

Snakes bears those animals
with death in their bellies
keeping them fed
through the long winter's sleep

do they imagine
coming out of it?

In the walled city
courtyards
lead into courtyards.
White chickens pitch
in wire baskets fighting
to stay alive.

I peel these oranges
from their rind
and the juice stays
on my hands.

I met a man today
who can't remember
what his first name was.

9

When I see numbers
in their forearms' flesh

when I walk backwards
so I cannot count

the Scrolls from Prague
ransomed
in a London attic

staring at handles
and the numbers stamped

"Reality, blind eye . . .
taught us to stare—"

Moths knock on my door
and I let them in
they are ashes
with wings
their eyes nine zeros
they are my cousins
staring at me.

10

There's a rim
to the universe Abba draws
limits—

running his fingers
on the saucer's edge
closing a circle
around the leftover
crumbs of cake

—the constellations
where we make
our choice.

Green rows of grapes
far as my eyes
until the vines end
and the sky begins

what vines there are
to hold the sky back.

Days
clear enough
to see the Dead Sea.

11

Rock of the dome
she said
not dome of the rock

the root of heaven
and the lid of hell

it boils
like a kettle of sun
over Mohammed's
footprint.

　　　　Abraham.
He stares at my bare
feet circling

blue grass lays tracks
across my arm

he would have sacrificed
his son

　　　I look
in the bush of shadow
for the ram.

The Burning of the Birds

Flight songs the way they build their nests—
all were miraculous.

Montezuma's water birds had ten lakes
emptied cleaned and refilled every day.
Salt water for sea birds
seven thousand feet high
and private pools for birds
from marshes and streams.

He could watch from the palace balcony
a ring of ibises herons flamingos
feeding at his gold-sandaled feet.

Hundreds of keepers cared for them
collecting molted feathers to make
bracelets and banners feathered fans
robes trailing shadows of the gods.

Bird-gods or god-birds shapes that flew
or skimmed the lakes like tropical flowers.
Sun was the quail or was the quail the sun?
Lord of them all the war god
beak of a bird's head covered with down.

And Cortes burned them
quetzals lovely cotingas hyacinth macaws.

To see how their wings like torches
filled with flame and remember that burning
every burning when the end is ashes
and the wings tip over in the smoke

to think of their pampered wings
the well-laid fire
how their colors flaked into it
beating against that brilliance till they fried

to hear the air scream their panic
turned into outrage into words
repeated like birds or seasons
or the outrage of history repeated
which is the same as fire or burning feathers.

Plumes of the quetzal
god-filled iridescence and the human blood
shriek in the air over and over
bright birds falling scorched
in the oven of their wings
as dead as any dream of paradise.

III

Gold pieces of ourselves . . .

Gone with the Popcorn

I set the table with model
airplanes, something to work on
while you eat the warmed-over food,
but I run out of glue
and it's too late to send down
to the hardware store for more.

We might have flown them
off the front porch
after dinner, watching them
glide under the sad trees
before it got too dark
to look for them.

The dark is always
sooner than we expected,
and I forget what I say
as soon as I say it. Like:
I don't want to get old
in traffic, or hold my hand.

So we go to see that old
movie again, and I cry
as I always do
when she comes home
to Tara just before
intermission. The war

is worse than ever,
soldiers bleeding all over
Atlanta, and I want
to make some profound
epigram about what
we don't learn from history.

But it gets personal.
I think I must be secretly
loving someone I can't
have, and why don't you
walk out on me saying
you don't give a damn?

Poem for a Gemini

In the mirror
leaves of the maple
aren't more than themselves.
The same ones behind me
shake at my window
as they keep shaking in the room.

Does a man dying on my TV
screen die twice?

Quick.
I get dizzy
watching the motion of things,
light in the veins.
And needing to tell it.
The green
like a light show
climbing my mind.

Fold the page double
and the ink repeats.

A new tree's growing
in the space between.

Head

One day I'm sitting on my nurse's lap
my small body with its hydrocephalic head
the legs drawn up and kicking
and no feet

       the nurse
trying to get my mouth in that great
hairless head to open.

            Now my mother
looking ancient waves her short arms:
don't give her that she's sick.

The nurse is furious:
what do you think it's for.

My mother's a hundred and two the sides
of her darling face cave in she wants
someone to read to her and I'm getting
all the attention.

           The pill's on my tongue
my head drops back like a huge lemon
hanging from its stem my eye-slits
water and I start to sneeze.

             That child
I hear them whisper that child's all
head

     and they abandon me.

In Touch

Be like a rock, you said,
to get the quality of rockness.
By the mere feeling you're in touch
with something else's center.
The seed moves in its original
darkness, hoarding light.
And past what's evident,
begins to breathe.

               Old celadon.
Vibrations. When you meet
somebody's stare while others talk,
and pass your secret anguish
through the room. He reels it in,
and flies a carrier pigeon back
with his own code. And you
decipher it, of course,
since it was only meant
for you.

             You know exactly
what he said. You think.
Giving him messages to send as if
he'd send them.

                It won't work.
Rocks blister in the weather
of your eye without your being
any part of them. He goes.
And you know
only what you know.

Signs

He had been planning to go back,
but slowly, as in the nightmare
where he missed the train, stopping
for traffic and the bridge washed out.

The way to her was moving
backward in the wrong direction.
He could not read the signs
with his new glasses,

and they kept changing.
Outside the city, fields
spread out like an aerial landscape
crossed by streams. He seemed

to be separate and whole.
That was not really what he wanted,
since he was used to making payments
every day, little by little

as a stone wears down. He knew
he was eaten away. But she
was only beautiful, she said,
because he told her.

He could see her at the door,
her face in the climbing roses,
and her hair, and the small light
in the hall like every morning.

The Performance

At intermission I find
you in the lobby
holding out chicken bones
for me to wish on.

Your eyes are steady
with accreditation.
They write off losses.
There are plenty.

On top of that a plot
to kill me, nothing
I have not known
from the beginning.

Someone is hiding
in one of the boxes,
hired, no doubt,
to follow me.

The great hall glitters,
and I won't go home.
Madeline is wearing
her diamond hair clip,

Beatrice swivels her
inherited opals,
rubies are thick
around Naomi's neck.

The house lights darken,
and I find my place,
crouch on the floor
to miss your aim.

The Performance

But everyone in the row
surrounds me.
Night after night,
we play it out again.

Subversion

All week the bees fall drowning in the pool,
and when you come home disguised as yourself,
I can't guess who you are.

Flies break their heads against
the floor-to-ceiling windows, and why
haven't you noticed the birds

burning on the brand-new barbecue,
leaves dropping in the middle of summer.
I remember the other men

in my life, how I hid little notes
to help them find me. In the piano.
Under my tongue. None

of them liked to read. You were an expert
in Slavic languages, studied the Talmud
as a child. Now

the cat's sick. She lies in the sun for hours
not blinking. While I'm trying to tell you
how I spend my days.

But you don't listen. You keep looking
for obsolete weapons in the glove
compartment of my ear.

Feeding Time in the Lion House

I'm tired of us all, the old,
the young, shaggy as lions are,
immaculate zoos. Of howls
in the throat, extravagant bellies
bringing up smoke. Day
after day, the same show,
thinking of blood, great
rivers of honey spilled
in the cage.

        The keeper arrives
without trumpets, any old
hero tossing it out.
Raw hunks of liver
speared in the trough. We sharpen
our grip in the flesh, measure
a width for jaws.

        The tongue
switches on! Pure as the rage
made pure as the slippery bones.

Lions. Our great yellow eyes
are the desert of deserts. I throw
my head in the way to catch
whole animals. Always
I rescue a piece of skin.

The Dream

after Dürer

You are dreaming yourself
into the sixteenth century
comfortably wedged between pillows
and a warm tile stove
while the devil in wings like a bat
squeezes a bellows at your ear.

You are dreaming yourself
into Venus with her hard nipples
and her hand stretched out
coaxing you to tickle her palm.

And maybe you even see Cupid
playing on stilts
with a Fortune ball.

You feel it throb in the dream.
Laziness is the Root of all Sin.
Virtue and Vice tug at both ends.

I am as pitiless as light
waking you
in a strange bed.

Michal

That wife unsettles me. Michal
at her window exhales propriety,
worries about appearances
while David jumps in the street.
Her David tearing off his clothes,
lifting his arms, their own
wild plumage, dancing for God!

Doesn't she know inside the Ark
the spirit gives off sparks?
Doesn't she know he has to
catch them on his skin, to leap
with each new pulse of fire?

The hills move back. The whole sky
stretches to make room. Gardens
explode. To bring God home!

He whirls. He bursts again
into the light, newborn
and not a King. As if
he still can choose his life,
run with the sheep.

                    What
will the neighbors say?
Her handmaids dance him to their beds.
Their hands are cool. He stays
with them.
                    Michal? He never
sleeps with her again.

Giving

She brings me warm bread
when she comes
bringing me wishes
in her face I want
over my own bones

now on the wet sand
at low tide
we look for perfect shells
and there are none

she puts
a sand dollar in my hand.

*

Rosewood bookends
from the family
fake amphora
things furniture

gold pieces
of ourselves each day
to bargain with
or trade

impurity of reason
it goes on
unreasonable

you never buy new
slippers or a hat
you like the old ones
broken in

Giving

sometimes at night
undressing
we look
turning from need
to love and out again

sometimes remember
that we used to speak
as we remembered
afterwards
to breathe.

*

The secret life
how we must keep
some shelter
even now

a tentative pressure
across the palm
an hour's heat of the body
recovered

rooms that we
come from return to
and not to each other

the fear of excesses
imagining courage
or what it's like
to give up
            this
to give.

*

Was it those summers
when I climbed
my knees raw
over the cracked bark

up to their tree house
with fruits or nuts or candy
so they'd let me in?

Their hands
opened
like jaws
crazy for meat.

*

Loving
transfigures

but my face that changes
when you change me
touching
is my own

it is as real as loneliness
or rain

and at the instant
when we give most
we fall deepest
into ourselves.

*

How we entreat
each other

giving

Giving

whatever there is
left

they would say
give us that
and let me in.

For Joan at Eilat

Mornings
with light still pale you drag
huge pipes around to soak
the date trees. Heat
begins to shimmer
on your skin. You watch
the crows go north. Is that
the way?

        You practice
flying like a small damp bird
brew herb tea in a suitcase
braid the steamed fragrance
in your hair

            and stand
in the clear water of the Red Sea
watching your toes. Branches
of coral. The water warm
near the edge of the desert.
You wade in it
as far as you can go.

PITT POETRY SERIES

Adonis, *The Blood of Adonis*
Jack Anderson, *The Invention of New Jersey*
Jon Anderson, *Death & Friends*
Jon Anderson, *Looking for Jonathan*
Gerald W. Barrax, *Another Kind of Rain*
Fazıl Hüsnü Dağlarca, *Selected Poems*
James Den Boer, *Learning the Way*
James Den Boer, *Trying to Come Apart*
Norman Dubie, *Alehouse Sonnets*
John Engels, *The Homer Mitchell Place*
Abbie Huston Evans, *Collected Poems*
Gary Gildner, *Digging for Indians*
Gary Gildner, *First Practice*
Michael S. Harper, *Dear John, Dear Coltrane*
Michael S. Harper, *Song: I Want a Witness*
Samuel Hazo, *Blood Rights*
Samuel Hazo, *Once for the Last Bandit: New and Previous Poems*
Shirley Kaufman, *The Floor Keeps Turning*
Shirley Kaufman, *Gold Country*
Abba Kovner, *A Canopy in the Desert*
Larry Levis, *Wrecking Crew*
Belle Randall, *101 Different Ways of Playing Solitaire and Other Poems*
Ed Roberson, *When Thy King Is A Boy*
Dennis Scott, *Uncle Time*
Richard Shelton, *Of All the Dirty Words*
Richard Shelton, *The Tattooed Desert*
David Steingass, *American Handbook*
David Steingass, *Body Compass*
Tomas Tranströmer, *Windows & Stones: Selected Poems*
Marc Weber, *48 Small Poems*
David P. Young, *Sweating Out the Winter*

COLOPHON

The type used to set these poems is Times Roman, a face originally cut for the London *Times*. It has since become a classic and is now the typeface most found in books and magazines. The Linotype version is employed here, with the printing directly from the type by Heritage Printers, Inc. The paper is Warren's Olde Style wove, an acid-free sheet designed to last more than 300 years. The design is by Gary Gore.